EDWARD ELGAR

Great is the Lord
Opus 67

for SATB and Organ or Orchestra

Psalm xlviii

Edited by Bruce Wood

NOVELLO

Published in Great Britain by Novello Publishing Limited
(a division of Music Sales Limited)
14/15 Berners Street, London W1T 3LJ

Exclusive distributors: Music Sales Limited, Newmarket Road
Bury St Edmunds, Suffolk, IP33 3YB
tel: +44 (0)1284 702600 fax +44 (0)1284 702592
Order No. NOV320067

www.chesternovello.com

Preface

Elgar began sketching *Great is the Lord* in late August 1910, but soon broke off, not to resume until March 1912, when he completed the vocal score in the space of a few days. The piece, published by Novello, was first performed on 12 July that year in Westminster Abbey, with organ accompaniment. There are numerous differences between the printed version and that given in the autograph score (London, British Library, Add. MS 58034, ff. 1-40); it was presumably while marking the proofs, which unfortunately have not survived, that Elgar made these revisions. Most of them affect only the markings, or amount to nothing more than judicious thickening of the organ part. Two changes, however, are more striking. The phrase-ending in bar 89 as given in the autograph is more abrupt, having the same rhythm as do the lower voices in bar 61; and the soaring soprano line in bars 172-175 proves – surprisingly – to have been an afterthought, all four voices originally being in unison, with the "big tune" confined to the organ part.

The textures of the organ writing strongly suggests that Elgar had orchestral accompaniment in mind from the first, but it was not until the February 1913 that he undertook the task of scoring the piece. In the process he further revised many details – some of them merely phrasing or articulation marks, but others affecting the notes themselves – with the result that some passages in the autograph full score (British Library, MS 58035, ff. 1-40) are not accurately represented by the organ part in the published vocal score. This new edition of the latter brings it into agreement with the orchestral score; besides emendations involving only the markings, there are changes to the notes in bars 16-17, 27, 41, 55, 70-71, 85, 92-95, 100, 104, 125, 127, 139-140, 148-149, 160, 176-177, and 197. The full score and orchestral material available on hire from the publishers have also been corrected from the autograph.

Both the vocal and the orchestral score are full of Elgar's characteristic markings of phrasing, articulation and expression, and of his highly specific directions as to flexibility of pulse, which he carefully distinguished from the main tempo indications. He was aware that some performers, especially singers, found his markings unduly restrictive. "Would you give yourself the trouble", he once wrote to W.G. McNaught of Novello, "to look over a proof [of some part-songs] with an eye – two eyes – to expression-marks and stage directions? I overdo this sort of thing (necessary in orchestral stuff) as I put down all my feelings as I write and then haven't the heart to take 'em out." For the attentive performer, nonetheless, Elgar's markings are as important as the notes themselves.

I am grateful to the Librarians and authorities of the British Library for their unfailing helpfulness, and for permission to consult materials among their holdings in the preparation of this new edition.

BRUCE WOOD
School of Music
University of Wales, Bangor
Summer 2004

To the Very Revd. The Dean of Wells (J. Armitage Robinson, D.D.) with sincere regard

GREAT IS THE LORD

Psalm xlviii

EDWARD ELGAR, Op. 67
Edited by Bruce Wood

sides of the north, the ci - ty, the ci - ty of the great King.

moun - tain of His ho - - li - ness.

moun - tain of His ho - - li - ness.

moun - tain of His ho - - li - ness.

God hath made Him-self known in her pal - a-ces for a re -

God hath made Him-self known in her pal - a-ces for a re -

God hath made Him-self known in her pal - a-ces for a re -

God hath made Him-self known in her pal - a-ces for a re -

45

- fuge, for a re - fuge. _____

- fuge.

- fuge.

- fuge.

D **Allegro moderato** ♪ = ♩ *of preceding movement*

50

mf ma molto marcato

For, lo! the kings as - sem - bled them - selves, they pass - ed by to-

For, lo! the kings as - sem - bled them - selves, they pass - ed by to-

For, lo! the kings as - sem - bled them - selves, they pass - ed by to-

For, lo! the kings as - sem - bled them - selves, they pass - ed by to-

D **Allegro moderato** ♪ = ♩ *of preceding movement*

50

Full Sw.
(closed)   *molto marcato*   *sempre staccato*   *cresc.*

f 8', 16', 32' *staccato*

8

14

midst of Thy tem - ple:___ as is Thy name. O God, so

is Thy praise un-to the ends___ of the earth, un-to the ends___ of the

earth; Thy right hand is full of right - - eous-ness, ___ Thy